W9-BTL-573

Arctic and Antarctic Life
Coloring Book

RUTH SOFFER

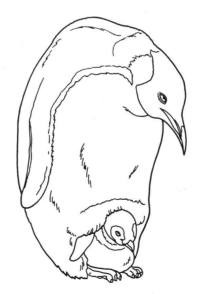

DOVER PUBLICATIONS, INC.
Mineola, New York

Copyright

Copyright © 1998 by Dover Publications, Inc.
All rights reserved under Pan American and International Copyright Conventions.

Bibliographical Note

Arctic and Antarctic Life Coloring Book is a new work, first published by Dover Publications, Inc., in 1998.

DOVER *Pictorial Archive* SERIES

This book belongs to the Dover Pictorial Archive Series. You may use the designs and illustrations for graphics and crafts applications, free and without special permission, provided that you include no more than ten in the same publication or project. (For permission for additional use, please write to: Dover Publications, Inc., 31 East 2nd Street, Mineola, N.Y. 11501.)

However, republication or reproduction of any illustration by any other graphic service, whether it be in a book or in any other design resource, is strictly prohibited.

International Standard Book Number: 0-486-29893-0

Manufactured in the United States of America
Dover Publications, Inc., 31 East 2nd Street, Mineola, N.Y. 11501

PUBLISHER'S NOTE

There are perhaps people who assume that because the Arctic and Antarctic are both polar regions, albeit at opposite ends of the globe, they must be similar in most respects. But there are, in fact, a good many differences between the Arctic and Antarctic, and what each contributes to the geological and biological diversity of the planet. The most obvious difference is that the Antarctic is a continent surrounded by an ocean, whereas the Arctic is an ocean basin surrounded by the northern parts of Europe, Asia, and North America, which almost encircle the Arctic sea. In addition, conditions in the Antarctic are usually more severe. It is the coldest, and perhaps the windiest, continent on Earth. The South Pole is covered by freshwater ice over a rock surface with a complex topography. In contrast, the North Pole is covered in sea ice floating on salt water, with the average temperature of the water being above freezing.

There are also major differences in the type of flora of the two regions. In order to find vegetation in the Antarctic in any way comparable to that found on the Arctic tundras, one would have to go north to the subantarctic islands. This obviously affects the distribution of fauna. With the exception of mammals introduced by humans, all mammals in the Antarctic are marine. Although there are relatively fewer species of marine mammals in the Antarctic than the Arctic, the actual numbers are larger in the Antarctic. When it comes to bird life, the Arctic species have, in the course of evolution, adapted to predators like the arctic fox, whereas the penguins of the Antarctic have never had to adapt to predators on land.

This book presents the animals of both polar regions, and it is hoped that these detailed illustrations will inspire further comparisons. To aid you, a number of drawings are shown in color on the covers, and alphabetical lists of common and Latin names appear in the front of the book.

ALPHABETICAL LIST OF COMMON NAMES

ALPHABETICAL LIST OF LATIN NAMES

Leopard Seal (*Hydrurga leptonyx*). A leopard seal on the ice presents no threat, but in the water it is an opportunistic hunter, patrolling the shoreline off rookeries where it preys on penguins. **Wilson's Petrel** (*Oceanites oceanicus*) flying above.

Weddell Seals *(Leptonychotes weddelli)* and pup in Antarctic. This seal has evolved to fill a very specific niche in the Antarctic ecosystem—the inshore fast-ice zone. This protects it from predation by killer whales, and it is able to exploit inshore prey for its own. It survives the winter by remaining in the warmer water below the ice, but must constantly maintain breathing holes in the crust of the ice.

Crab-Eater Seals *(Lobodon carcinophagus)*. This is the most abundant Antarctic seal. In spite of its name, it does not in fact eat crabs, but krill, the tiny shrimp-like crustaceans that blue whales eat. As it swims, its elaborately shaped molars screen the krill out of the water.

Walrus *(Odobenus rosmarus)*. Walruses live in large herds, and move seasonally based on the advance and retreat of ice packs. The tusks of the walrus can grow up to three feet in length.

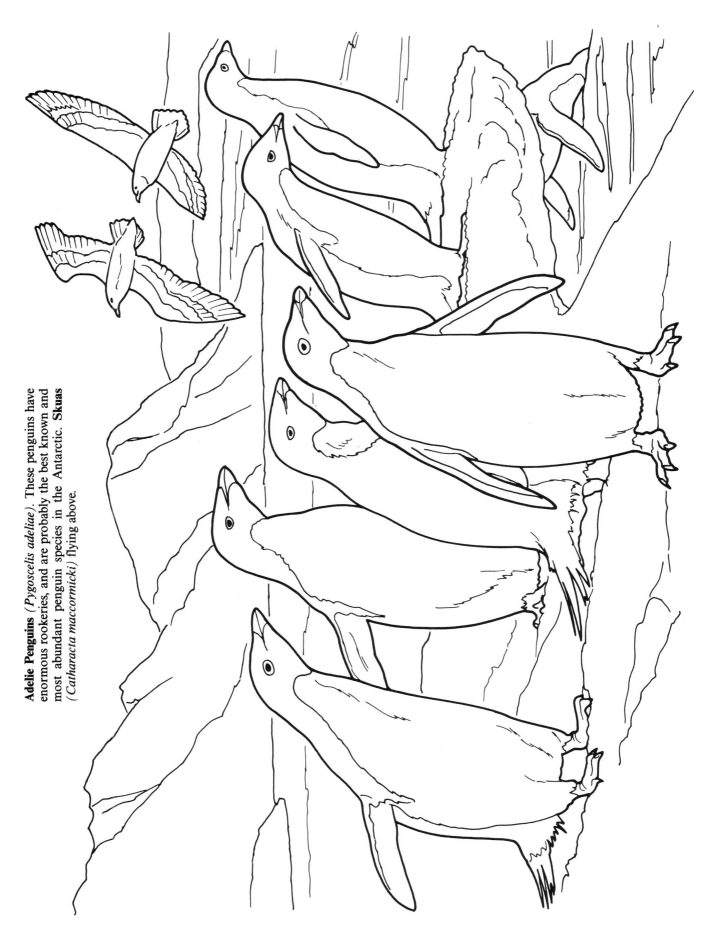

Adelie Penguins (*Pygoscelis adeliae*). These penguins have enormous rookeries, and are probably the best known and most abundant penguin species in the Antarctic. **Skuas** (*Catharacta maccormicki*) flying above.

Rockhopper Penguin *(Eudyptes crestatus)*. Whereas most penguins walk or stroll, this species hops. They can be seen nesting on steep slopes, where they build up the downhill side with vegetation to form a comfortable platform. Their heads are crowned by black and yellow tufts.

Emperor Penguin (*Aptenodytes forsteri*). Among birds, the emperor penguin is definitely unique. It is the only species to breed exclusively along the edge of the Antarctic Continent, and the only one that lays eggs in the seemingly forbidding circumstance of an Antarctic winter.

Gentoo Penguins (*Pygoscelis papua*). These birds nest on low flat areas where their large nests of pebbles are spaced just beyond pecking distance from their neighbors. The

Blue-Eyed Shags (*Phalacrocorax atriceps*) are capable of diving to depths of at least 25 meters.

Chinstrap Penguin *(Pygoscelis antarctica)*. The narrow band of black-tipped feathers under the chin make this handsome species easy to identify.

Polar Bear (*Ursus maritimus*), and cub in the Arctic. The polar bear can outrun a reindeer for short distances on land, and while reindeer are found in the bear's diet, its preferred habitat is pack ice, where it feeds primarily on the ringed seal.

King Penguin *(Aptenodytes patagonicus)*. Closely related to the Emperor, the King Penguin is shorter and half the weight, and has brighter yellow coloration.

Southern Elephant Seal (*Mirounga leonina*). Hunted to critical levels in the nineteenth century for its oil, the southern elephant seal is now recovered, and extending its range to former breeding colonies.

12

Steller Sea Lion *(Eumetopias jubata)*. This gregarious sea lion of the Bering Sea is golden brown in color. Although its weight makes it clumsy on land, it is a graceful swimmer.

Snowy Owl *(Nyctea scandiaca)*. This large white owl lives on the open Arctic tundra, making its nest on the ground. It preys chiefly on **Lemmings** *(Lemmus sibiricus)*, in background.

14

Black-Browed Albatross *(Diomedea melanophris)*. Since the first voyages to Antarctica, the grace and power of the flight of the Albatross have been commented upon by explorers and poets alike. They spend the greater part of their lives in the air, and have such an efficient flying technique that they expend the least amount of energy in traveling vast distances. **Humpback Whale's** flukes in background.

Dall Sheep *(Ovis dallii)* prefer rough high terrain like the Brooks Range in Alaska, where there is little competition for food. **Purple Saxifrage** *(Saxifraga oppositifolia)* in front, grows as far north as land extends.

Atlantic Puffins *(Fratercula corniculata)*. Also called the common puffin, this is the only east coast variety. Its range extends as far south as Maryland. **Arctic Poppies** *(Papaver lapponicum)*, a favorite food of the muskox.

Muskox *(Ovibos moschatus)*, called *Oomingmak* by Eskimos, on the Arctic tundra. The muskox has a coarse dark brown coat of outer hair, and a soft, fine inner coat that is so dense neither cold nor frost can penetrate it.

Arctic Wolf, subspecies of Gray Wolves *(Canis lupus)*. The wolf has the largest range of any terrestrial mammal outside of humans. The large size of the arctic wolf, combined with its penchant for socializing in packs, makes it perfectly adapted to preying on large species of Arctic wildlife.

Caribou/Reindeer *(Rangifer tarandus)*. The caribou is a member of the deer family, and is believed to have emigrated from Siberia via the Bering land bridge. In many places on the tundra, domesticated reindeer exist in the same general range as the wild caribou. **White Cotton Grass** *(genus Eriophorum)* in foreground.

Gyr Falcon *(Falco rusticolus)*. This Arctic predator preys chiefly on other birds. Plumages vary throughout its range from white to dark, barred or unbarred tail feathers.

Lapland Longspur *(Calcarius lapponicus)*, and **Pasque Flowers** *(genus Anemone)* on the Alaskan tundra. The blooms of the pasque flowers may be white or purple.

Arctic Hare *(Lepus arcticus)*. Normally solitary creatures, these animals have also been seen in large herds of several hundred individuals. Gray (Arctic) Wolf looking on.

Arctic Fox *(Alopex lagopus)*. This animal can have a winter coat of white or dark bluish-gray, depending on the phase.

Their dens can have as many as 12 entrances, and a network of tunnels covering about 30 square meters.

Arctic Terns *(Sterna paradisaea)*. **Humpback Whales**
(Megaptera novaeangliae) in background—whose flippers
are nearly a third as long as its body.

Killer Whale *(Orcinus orca)*. Killer whales tend to travel in groups (called pods), of up to 30 individuals. In some areas fishermen resent the competition they get from killer whales, who feed on commercially important fish like salmon. Seals are also an important part of the killer whale's diet.

Narwhal *(Monodon monoceros)*. Scientists believe the distinctive long tusk of the male is used for sparring during the mating season.

Beluga Whales (*Delphinapterus leucas*) in the Arctic. Also known as white whales, for their pure white coloring. Killer whales are probably their primary predator, but polar bears are also a threat to these small whales.

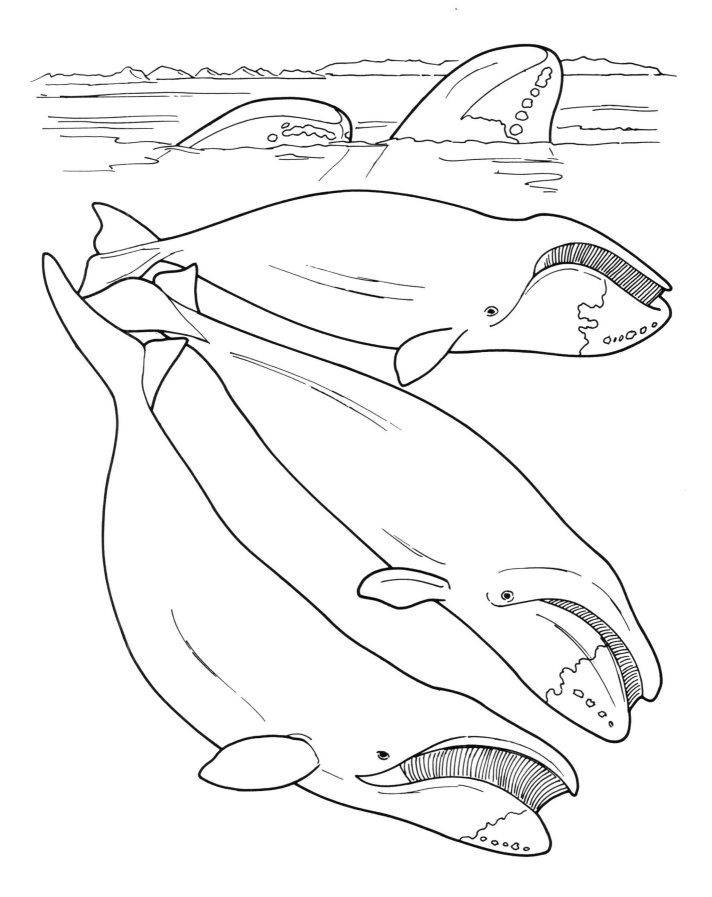

Bowhead Whales *(Balaena mysticetus)*. These whales are almost completely black, except for a white chin patch.

Minke Whale (*Balaenoptera acutorostrata*). These whales tend to be solitary, sometimes seen in pairs, but rarely in large groups. The most conspicuous marking is a diagonal white band on each flipper.

Sei Whale *(Balaenoptera borealis)*. These whales are generally skimming near the surface, where they feed on plankton, schooling fish, and squid.

Pygmy Right Whale (*Caperea marginata*). Only a few dozen of this species have been examined by scientists, and sightings are rare, so little is known about the natural history of this creature. Its shyness may be a benefit, as it has never been exploited, except as an incidental result of netting operations.

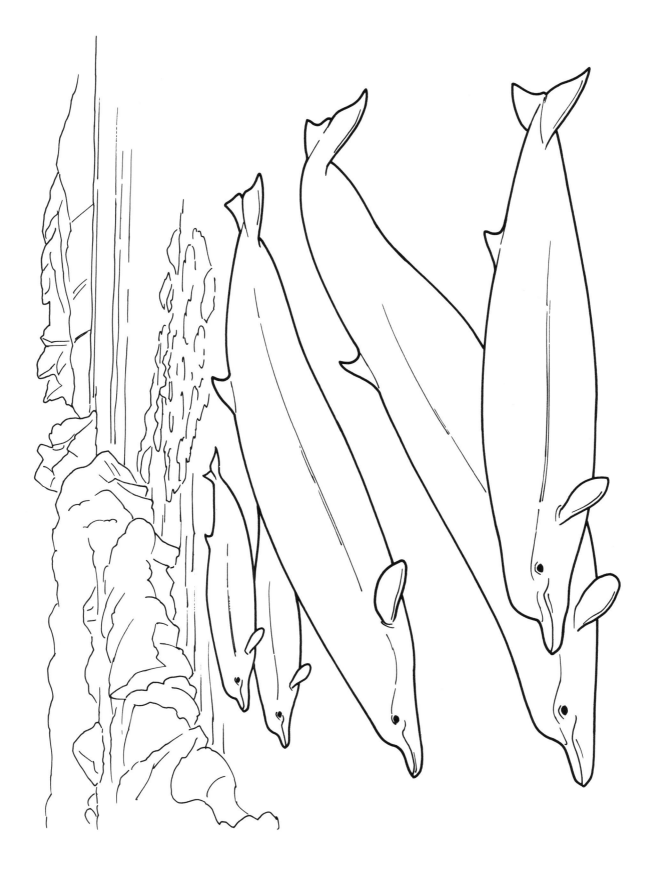

Baird's Beaked Whale (*Berardius bairdii*). This is the largest of the beaked whales, growing to nearly 13 meters in length.

Ringed Seal *(Phoca hispida)* in breathing hole. Polar bear in background, whose favorite food is the ringed seal.

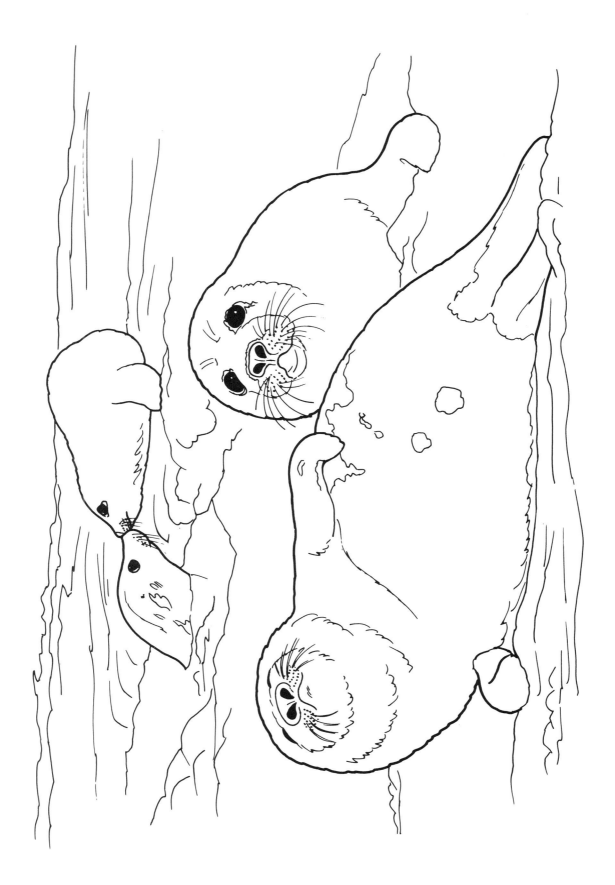

Baby Harp Seals (*Phoca greonlandica*) in front, with mother harp nuzzling her baby in background.

Willow Ptarmigan *(Lagopus nivalis)*. Shown here in winter plumage, the willow ptarmigan probably has the most specialized diet of any animal in the Arctic, since during the winter months up to 94 percent of its diet may consist of willow buds.

Butterfly *(genus Boloria)*. Alaska—Summer tundra. Daisy bloom in front (yellow). Wild geranium in background (lavender).

Antarctica undersea. Top: Emperor Penguins diving. Front Left: **Crinoids** *(Nemaster rubiginosa)* on Volcano Sponge. Top Center: Desmonema can be 3 ft. in diameter. Right: **Pycnogonis Sea Spider** *(Phoxichilidium maxilare)*.

Parasitic Jaeger *(Stercorarius parasiticus).* Also called
Arctic Skua.

Emperor Goose *(Chen canagica)*. This small Arctic goose has gray silver plumage, edged in black and white, which gives it a distinctive scaled effect. Tufted saxifrage in foreground.

Sun Star Anemones (of the order *Actiniaria*) in Arctic waters. Narwhal whales in background.

Left Front: **Sea Snail** (genus *Janthinidae*). Top Left: **Lions Mane Jellyfish**. Right: **Frilly Nunibranch**.

Black Guillemot *(Cepphus grylle)*. This bird is colored black with a white patch on the wings, and has bright red feet. The guillemot is an excellent swimmer, and is usually seen close to shorelines.

King Eider *(Somateria spectabilis)*. Two males in foreground, three females in background. Eiders provide eiderdown filling for pillows and comforters. A pound of down can be harvested from every 35-40 nests without interrupting breeding cycles.